Morayshire's Railways
including Inverness-shire and the north
in photographs by ENC Haywood

Kyle of Lochalsh Station a former 'Devon Belle' observation car at the end of a train for Inverness, July 1961.

© Stenlake Publishing, ENC Haywood, 2024
First published in the United Kingdom, 2024,
54-58 Mill Square,
Catrine, KA5 6RD
by Stenlake Publishing Ltd.
www.stenlake.co.uk

ISBN 978-1-84033-978-9

The publishers regret that they cannot supply copies of any pictures featured in this book.

Printed by
P2D Books, 1 Newlands Rd, Westoning, Bedford MK45 5LD

Plaque of the Inverness and Aberdeen Junction Railway arms which was fixed to the viaduct over the River Spey commemorating the completion of the railway to Keith. Photographed in Inverness Station in July 1961.

Introduction

The Morayshire Railway was the first line to be constructed north of Aberdeen. The railway from Elgin to Lossiemouth was approved in 1845, but owing to the difficult financial climate caused by the Railway Mania wouldn't be completed until 1852.

In 1846 the Great North of Scotland Railway was proposed, a trunk route that would connect Aberdeen to Inverness passing through Elgin on the way. It too struggled to raise capital and it took until 1854 for a curtailed line to be built from Kittybrewster to Huntly, a long way short of Elgin, let alone Inverness.

To the west, unimpressed by the Great North of Scotland's progress, Inverness interests sought to establish their own railway connection to the rest of the UK. In 1853 they promoted the Inverness and Nairn Railway, which was fiercely opposed by the Great North of Scotland. However, after the right to run trains over the new line was offered the objection was withdrawn and the railway approved the following year. A few months later newspapers carried articles on the proposed Inverness & Elgin Junction Railway, which would continue the line from Nairn eastward and join the Morayshire Railway in Elgin. In February 1855 the directors of the proposed line met with those of the Great North of Scotland, and were persuaded to shelve their plans. By August the promoters of the plan revived and renamed it as the Inverness and Aberdeen Junction Railway. The new line would extend from Nairn to the Spey where it would meet the Great North of Scotland Railway. The latter company had recently received approval to extend its line from Huntly to Keith, from there it was expected to extend to the river. However, as the plans developed it was agreed that the Inverness and Aberdeen Junction Railway would continue their line to Keith, and there the two lines met in 1858. There was now a connection from Inverness to the south, but a more direct link to the rest of Scotland was seen as desirable. To this end the Inverness and Perth Junction railway was proposed. It would head south from Nairn, later changed to Forres to suit fishing interests, and head over the moors of western Morayshire to Speyside then onwards through the mountains to Perth.

In the meantime the Morayshire Railway, in fact even before it laid a single rail, had resolved to build an extension to Craigellachie. Instead of constructing their own continuous line they intended their extension to be a branch from the Great North of Scotland once its line reached Elgin. The Morayshire would then run services over the other company's line to their branch. In the end their plan came to fruition using the line of the Inverness and Aberdeen Junction Railway's instead. Services to a terminus on the north bank of the Spey began a few days after the line to Keith was opened. Disagreements with, and restrictions imposed by, the other company quickly led the Morayshire Railway to construct their own line to Craigellachie, which was completed in 1862.

By that time the Great North of Scotland had funded and constructed the Keith and Dufftown Railway and was in the process of completing the Speyside Railway to Boat of Garten. Its own Craigellachie Station would be sited on the south bank of the River Spey, and in 1863 a bridge was constructed that would allow it to use the Morayshire Railway to run trains into Elgin.

A series of railways were promoted to construct a line north from Inverness, each connecting and extending from the previous one. The first, the Inverness and Ross-shire Railway, was proposed in 1862 and reached Wick and Thurso with the completion of the Sutherland and Caithness Railway in 1874. In 1865 the Dingwall and Skye railway was promoted to connect Inverness and Kyle of Lochalsh. It was beset with difficulties and in the end only got as far as Stromeferry. It would take another 27 years before the intended terminus at Kyle of Lochalsh was reached.

ENC Haywood, who lived in Nottingham, had relatives in Aberdeen and spent many short breaks there. He would often travel by indirect routes between the cities occasionally stopping to take photographs as he went. He also would break his journey to stay for a day or two along the route, taking the opportunity to travel on lines like those to Wick and Kyle of Lochalsh before continuing to Aberdeen or Nottingham.

Boat of Garten, June 1954.

Boat of Garten, June 1954.

Broomhill Junction, the divergence point of the two lines through Speyside, April 1964.. The Speyside Railway curves to the right, the train is headed on the line to Forres. There was no actual junction at this point, to save on the cost of a signal box and manning it, the lines began to run parallel from here to Boat of Garten almost three miles to the south-west.

Grantown-on-Spey (East) with No. 62268 heading towards Aviemore, June 1954.

Ballindalloch, April 1964.

Craigellachie, shortly before closure in April 1968.

Spey Bridge at Craigellachie, April 1968.

Looking south from Rothes Station, April 1968.

Exchanging a token for access to the single track section north of Rothes. April 1968.

Longmorn Station, April 1968. The station building stood on the west side of the tracks.

Longmorn, April 1968, the passing loop through the station lifted in anticipation of the closure of the line.

The Great North of Scotland's station in Elgin (East), April 1968. The station was remodelled in 1902 giving three bay platforms for terminating services and one through platform, seen on the right.

The departure board at Elgin East, April 1968. Platforms 5 and 6 were located at the nearby Elgin (West). To the right of the board is the Withdrawal of Railway Passenger Service Notice, informing passengers of what is about to be lost, and the bus services provided by W Alexander & Sons (Northern) which served the communites that would no longer be accessable by rail.

The main entrance and booking hall of Elgin (East), April 1968.

Exterior of Elgin (East). The entrance to the booking hall is under the glass canopy, the door hidden by the wing of the building, April 1968.

Exterior of Elgin (East) from Station Road, April 1968. Part of the goods yard is on the left. A little less than 200 metres to the right was Elgin (West) Station.

Elgin (West) Station in April 1968. The station was modernised in 1968/69, raising the platforms. During the work eastbound services were initially diverted to the recently-closed Elgin (East) station, requiring trains to reverse back onto the main line after visiting. In 1990 the station was completely rebuilt and nothing remains of these old buildings.

Looking east from the platform of Elgin (West), April 1968. The turret of Elgin (East) is on the left. The junction and connecting lines between the stations veer left; those straight on continue to Aberdeen.

Looking from the end of the platform to the bridge over the lines to Aberdeen from Elgin (West), April 1968.

Lossie Junction seen from the cab of a Moray Coast service, April 1962.

Approaching the Spey Viaduct from the west, April 1962.

Lossiemouth looking south, April 1964.

Lossiemouth Station buildings and goods shed, April 1964.

Looking south past the goods shed and station building at Lossiemouth, April 1964. The line passing on the left served the Inner Basin of Lossiemouth Harbour, just off to the left.

Broomhill Station on the Forres to Speyside line, April 1964.

Dava Station, April 1964. The station wasn't quite as desolate as this photograph of the east platform suggests. The station building was on the opposite side.

Looking south, back along the line to Dava, from Forres Station, April 1964.

No. 57587 by the Loco Box signal box and locomotive works, on the eastern approach to Inverness Station, July 1961.

Inverness Station, July 1961.

Inverness Station from the platforms, July 1961.

Inverness coaling hopper is on the right and the curve of the roundhouse engine shed pokes above the top of No. 54491, July 1961.

No. 1649 was transferred from the Bristol area in 1957 to work on the Dornoch Branch. It remained in the Highlands after the branch closed until it was withdrawn in 1962. For much of that time it was based at Dingwall where it was photographed in July 1961.

The remote Glencarron Platform, July 1961.

Train winding its way back towards Inverness along the Kyle of Lochalsh extension, July 1961

Kyle of Lochalsh Station, July 1961.

Returning to the line north from Dingwall at Lairg where a Sutherland Transport and Trading Company bus waits to take passengers to Lochinver.

Borrobol Platform, July 1961.

Georgemas Junction looking west towards the junction, with a Wick-bound train facing the camera, July 1961.

The northern platform and station house at Georgemas Junction on a Thurso-bound train, July 1961.

Wick Locomotive Shed, July 1961.

No. 54482 in Wick Locomotive Shed, July 1961.

Photographed from the turntable, the locomotive shed is to the left, the goods yard is on the right and the goods shed on the far right. The passenger station at Wick is further to the right not in the photograph. Looking back down the line towards Georgemas Junction, July 1961.

No. 54482 outside the locomotive shed at Wick, July 1961.

Hoy Station, on the way to Thurso, July 1961.